About This Book

Title: *Look at the Graph*

Step: 3

Word Count: 196

Skills in Focus: Digraph ph

Tricky Words: charts, line, numbers, connect, sketch, tool, change, down, make, sides

Ideas For Using This Book

Before Reading:

- **Comprehension:** Look at the title and cover image together. Ask readers what they know about graphs. What new things do they think they might learn in this book?
- **Accuracy:** Practice saying the tricky words listed on page 1.
- **Phonics and Phonemic Awareness:** Tell students they will read words with digraphs. Explain that a digraph is two letters that make one sound. Have students listen as you segment the sounds in the word *graph* (/g/, /r/, /a/, /f/). Ask students to identify what the word is and where the /f/ sound is heard in the word. Is it at the beginning, middle, or end? Point to the word *graph* in the title. Help readers see that the /f/ is at the end, made by the letter combination *ph*. Repeat with the word *long* (where does the reader hear *ng*?) and *this* (where do they hear *th*?).

During Reading:

- Have readers point under each word as they read it.
- **Decoding:** If readers are stuck on a word, help them say each sound and blend the sounds together smoothly. Be sure to point out any digraph letter combinations.
- **Comprehension:** Invite students to talk about what new things they are learning about graphs while reading. What are they learning that they didn't know before?

After Reading:

Discuss the book. Some ideas for questions:

- Have you ever read a graph? What kind of graphs have you seen before?
- What do you still wonder about graphs?

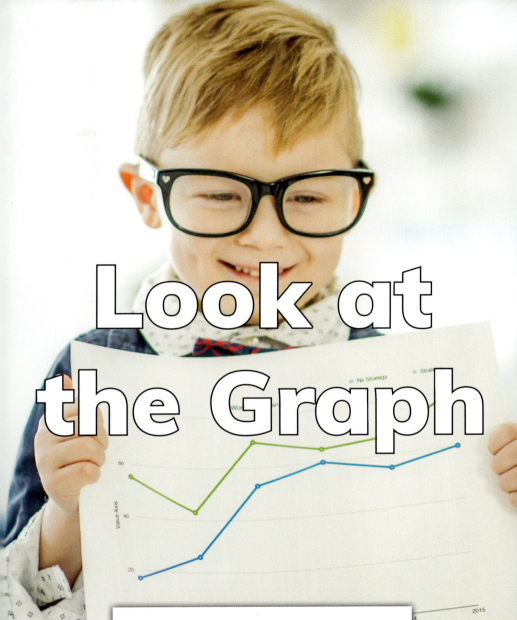

Look at the Graph

Text by Laura Stickney

Reading Consultant
Deborah MacPhee, PhD
Professor, School of Teaching and Learning
Illinois State University

PICTURE WINDOW BOOKS
a capstone imprint

In math class, you can learn to read graphs. A graph is a math tool.

Graphs are charts that show data.

Graphs can help us see patterns.

Graphs can have 2 sides.

The graph's x-axis is long.
The graph's y-axis is tall.

Bar graphs help us see when this has more than that.

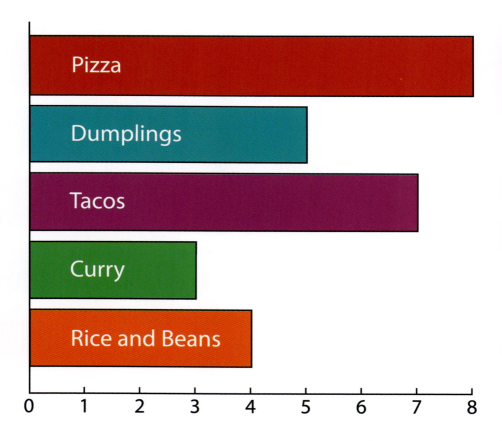

Favorite Foods in Ms. Jimenez's Class

Number of Students

Line graphs have dots. They help us see how things change.

Average High Temperature by Month

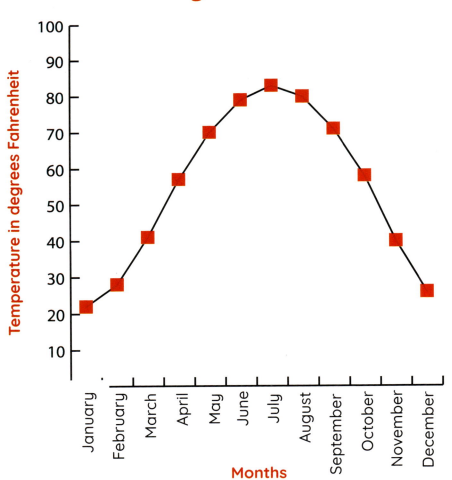

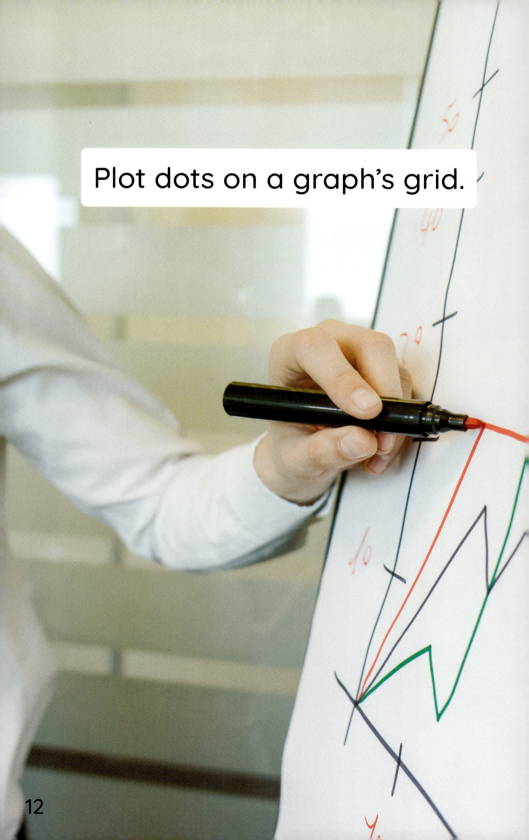

Plot dots on a graph's grid.

Then connect the graph's dots with a line. Does the path of dots go up or down?

Phlox is a plant. It has buds.

Graphs can tell the number of buds on a phlox.

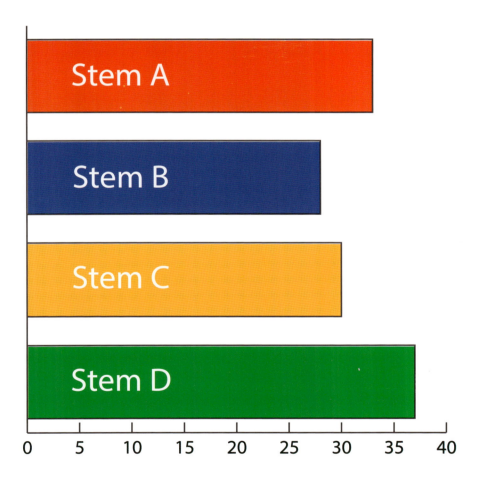

30.053	-0.092486	70.039	
27.195	0.01008	72.795	0.
30.691	-0.21527	69.524	
26.567	0.31829	73.115	-0
30.293	-0.20549	69.912	-0.
28.544	-0.11917	71.575	-0
26.948	0.074281	72.977	-0
29.397	-0.18033	70.784	-0
26.15	-0.10527	73.955	-0
31.592	-0.1296	68.538	-0
28.559	-0.14906	71.59	-0
27.309	-0.20186	72.892	-
29.008	-0.034277	71.026	-0

This is a long list of numbers. Phil cannot tell if there is a pattern.

This is a graph. Phil can tell there is a pattern!

To make a graph, get a set of data. You can ask kids which they like, dolphins or fish.

Use the data to sketch a graph.

The red part of the graph will show how many kids said fish.

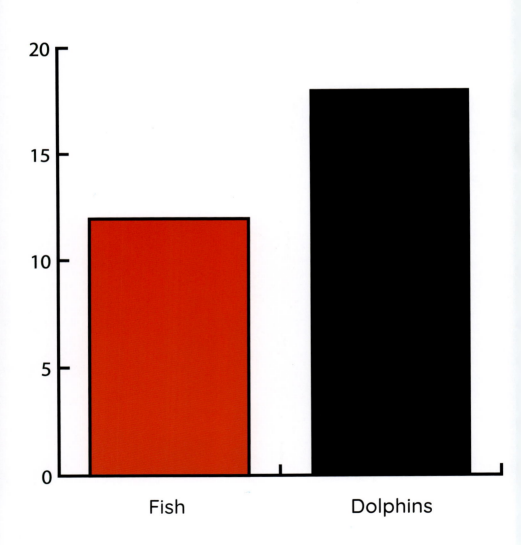

The black part of the graph will show how many said dolphins. Which do kids like best?

Graphs are fun! What graph will you sketch, math whiz?

More Ideas:

Phonemic Awareness Activity

Practicing Digraphs:
Write the story words *graph, math*, and *this*. Have readers tap out the sounds down their arm, starting by their shoulders. Ask readers how many sounds they hear in the word. Remind them that the *p* and *h* make one sound when they are together, even though they are two letters. The *t* and *h* make one sound when they are together too. Continue with other *ph*, *wh*, and *th* story words, such as *dolphin, which, when, math, whiz*, and *phlox*.

Extended Learning Activity

Let's Make a Graph:
Help readers collect a simple set of data. Then ask readers to use that data to create their own bar graph or line graph. After students have created their graphs, ask them to write three sentences about their graphs. Challenge students to use words with *ph*, *wh*, *th*, and *ch* letter combinations in their sentences.

Published by Picture Window Books, an imprint of Capstone
1710 Roe Crest Drive, North Mankato, Minnesota 56003
capstonepub.com

Copyright © 2026 by Capstone.
All rights reserved. No part of this publication may be reproduced in whole or in part, or stored in a retrieval system, or transmitted in any form or by any means, electronic, mechanical, photocopying, recording, or otherwise, without written permission of the publisher.

Library of Congress Cataloging-in-Publication Data is available on the Library of Congress website.

ISBN: 9798875227080 (hardback)
ISBN: 9798875230158 (paperback)
ISBN: 9798875230134 (eBook PDF)

Image Credits: Capstone: Karon Dubke, 6–7; iStock: FatCamera, 3, 24, JDawnInk, 8–9, mrPliskin, cover, uschools, 19, vaitekune, 14, Vergani_Fotografia, 4–5, WhitneyLewisPhotography, 1, 18; Red Line Editorial: 10, 11, 15, 20; Shutterstock: Eugenio Marongiu, 12–13, fizkes, 17, Ra17, 16, Zurijeta, 22–23

Printed and bound in China. 6274